The Solution Focused Marriage

5 SIMPLE HABITS THAT WILL BRING OUT THE BEST IN YOUR RELATIONSHIP

ELLIOTT CONNIE

Printed in the United States of America
First Printing, 2013
ISBN 978-0-578-12699-9

The Connie Institute
1660 Keller Parkway
Suite 102
Keller, TX 7248
www.TheConnieInstitute.com

This book is dedicated to all of the couples that have visited my office over the years. You have all demonstrated the true power of love and relationships.

Acknowledgements

I don't know exactly how my fascination with relationships and marriage started, but at some point I became passionate about helping people to make the changes in their relationship that help them move closer together and further away from problems.

I am grateful to the people that have helped me along the way, not just with this book but also to the mentors that have helped me learn to apply the Solution Focused Approach in couples therapy.

Linda Metcalf, I am forever grateful that you took the time to teach me. Thank you from the deepest part of my heart; I am forever your student. Chris Iveson, from the first time we met, it was clear that I was looking at someone that was interested in the same thing that I was when working with clients. Thank you for letting me study with you ever since that first meeting. Harvey Ratner and Evan George, our conversations about this approach have been priceless! However, your brotherhood has meant even more to me. Thank you.

There are several people that played such an integral role in this book being written that it would not have happened without them. Lesley Worsham, thank you for your dedication and continued support. I honestly don't know where I would be without you. Dan Crandall, you took time out of your busy schedule to proof read and edit this project and make it the best it could be, thank you. To all of my staff, your hard work and support help me to focus while you all worked so hard to prevent the distractions from interrupting me, thank you all for that.

Table of Contents

Preface

"Falling in love consists merely in uncorking

the imagination and bottling the common sense."

—HELEN ROWLAND

The need for this book has become more and
more apparent to me over the years of working with
couples as a therapist. In fact, from the time I was a
young child, I have paid attention to relationships and
what made them succeed and what caused them to fail.
This was due to the fact that I watched my own mother
and father spend years having horrible arguments and
even physical fights. In short, it was rough. I would see
the relationships that my friends' parents seemed to

have. I would see their parents holding hands, expressing love through warm touches and kind words. I could not help but wonder, "why isn't this how my parents are?" From that time in my life, my fascination with couples' relationships began.

Years later, I was presented with the opportunity to pursue an education and career in counseling. However, my childhood became a deterrent. I was so uncomfortable with the idea of working with couples that I tried to steer clear of that work. I had watched my mother and father have so many arguments that just the thought of sitting in a room where an argument might break out made me incredibly uncomfortable.

Upon my graduation, I got the chance to work at a local mental health agency that focused on working with children. It was perfect!

I wrongfully assumed that because the focus of this location was children, my discomfort with working with couples would be avoidable here. On my very first day of work, during a staff meeting, my boss mentioned that couples did, in fact, come to this agency for counseling. I panicked. I immediately approached the person who was in charge in handing out the referrals to the therapists and asked her not to send any couples to me. I begged and begged! I let her know that I would be happy to see any other referral that came into the office. Send me the most challenging children and even the most disruptive families. She agreed and I thought I was in the clear. Little did I know that the philosophy of this agency was to present new therapists with situations that would challenge them and cause them to grow. As a result of this, the very first referral form that was sent to me was for a couple ... UGH!

At the time I was upset with the agency not listening to my request, but soon I became very thankful.

As the date of this first session approached, I was

concerned. I envisioned this couple coming to my office with their marriage in distress, looking to me for help, and to be honest, I did not feel prepared. I was stressed that I would not have the words to be helpful. I also was very aware of my fear of couples arguing and also envisioned the couple screaming at each other and me running out of the room screaming, as well. I began to research couples therapy fervently. I read books and talked to more seasoned clinicians until I felt I was ready.

When the first couple finally arrived, that old feeling of fascination about couples' relationships returned and immediately I fell in love with working with couples. From that very first session, I was launched into a journey that reconnected me with my childhood fascination.

Since that time, I have spent years focusing my work on couples therapy, writing books about working with couples and traveling the world teaching clinicians to work with couples. It has truly been an amazing ride. I have worked with tens of thousands of couples and have begun to answer the question that has puzzled me since my childhood: what makes some couples successful and other couples unsuccessful?

I have found that there are certain, very specific habits that lead to long-term success. This book will share those habits and practices with you and allow you to be able to apply these lessons to your relationship immediately.

Introduction

"A loving heart is the beginning of all knowledge."

—THOMAS CARLYLE

The idea for this book came to me as a result of my work with clients. In truth, I never sought to write books. My dream was always to provide couples counseling in order to help people have a more enjoyable relationship experience. It has been an absolute blast and truly such an honor. Over the years, many of the couples with which I have worked expressed the need for a book that would help them along the way after counseling. It was because of these couples that the idea for this book was born.

The best way for me to start is to introduce and

explain the type of therapy that I use in my work with couples, as it is the foundation of the skills highlighted in this book. Known as Solution Focused Brief Therapy (SFBT), this form of therapy is very different from traditional forms of psychotherapy. SFBT invites clients to work towards creating their desired future as opposed to removing a particular problem.

I will never forget the moment I first heard about this way of working with clients. I was a young graduate student, and I was a having a very difficult time with the course work. The issue was not that the work was too challenging; instead, it was that I was not getting excited about what I was learning about working with clients. When I entered the counseling program, I was hoping to inspire people and help people live happier lives. I had the idea that I would be able to touch people's lives and this was the driving force behind my desire to learn about the field of psychotherapy. As I learned more about the field of psychotherapy, it became increasingly clear to me that my personal philosophies did not fit the mold of the traditional, problem-focused forms of therapy that I was learning. In fact, I felt so strongly that I made the decision to quit graduate school.

I was lost.

I will never forget coming home and telling my fiancée that I did not think that I was cut out to be a therapist. Talking to people about their problems and identifying their flaws as a means of helping them simply did not fit with me. Thankfully, my future wife said something that put me back on track and ultimately changed my life. "I will not marry a quitter," she declared. I was absolutely stunned. I expected her to say something empathetic or nurturing (in the subsequent years of marriage to her, I am no longer surprised by the answer she gave).

It was the middle of the semester, and I was

attempting to quit immediately, but after my fiancée's less-than-warm comment, I decided that I would have to, at least, finish out the semester. I was not happy in school, but I most certainly was not interested in losing my fiancée. I asked her if completing the semester was enough for her and thankfully she agreed.

The following week, everything changed.

I was so relieved, as I was no longer focused on becoming a therapist; I was just trying to last the semester so I could move on and figure out what career shift I could make. I will never forget walking into my first class of the week. I was finally relaxed and took my normal seat in the back of the class. Then it happened. Instead of the professor beginning to review the topic for that week, the director of the program addressed our class and introduced a new professor who would begin teaching the following semester. As part of her introduction, the new professor began to describe the way she worked with clients and I was stunned. She shared a story of working with an adolescent girl who was struggling to overcome depression. As she talked, it was clear to me that she was not simply assessing this client for problems; she was doing something very different. She seemed to believe in her client, and she seemed to be curious about the strengths of this young woman and what her talents were. I was amazed. The newly-hired professor completed her brief introduction, calmly collected her things and exited the room. I knew I had to learn more.

Something about what she was doing made complete and total sense to me. I was so excited about what had just occurred that I knew I had to stay in school to learn more about this process of focusing on solutions. Instantly, I had hope that I could be a counselor if there was a way of helping clients that was respectful and led by the client's goals, not the therapist's. The following semester, I took the course offered by the new professor I had met that night, and my journey towards solution land had begun.

Upon my graduation, it was time to start looking for a job. As mentioned, I found a job working at an agency and off I went to work with clients and, of course, couples. There, I was met with a new hurdle. I realized that, in order to be successful in this agency, and in this field, I was going to have to develop skills to work with couples. I was excited. I was beginning to reconnect with my childhood ambitions of helping couples, but I ran into another small hurdle. While there was an extraordinary large amount of training materials on the solution-focused approach in general, there was very little available on applying this approach to working with couples. Undeterred, I set out to become the best couples therapist I could be. I fell in love with this work. I began taking notes along the way about how I was building conversations with couples and how I was applying the solution-focused approach to couples therapy. My book of notes became my Bible, and it came everywhere with me. I was constantly adding to it and reading from it.

As my confidence and ability grew, I decided to leave the agency and start my own counseling practice where I could focus on my work with couples. In the next few years, I became busier than I ever imagined, seeing clients, the majority of whom were couples, in my office. I have seen couples that were in the direst of situations, dealing with infidelity, intimacy issues, arguing, fighting and many other challenges that marriages face today. I worked with couples that were, quite literally, one step away from divorce and, in some cases, the divorce proceedings had already been initiated by one or both of the partners. It has been the hardest work I have ever done, but also the most rewarding.

After a while, I started to notice that, regardless of

the challenges that faced each couple when they came into my office, things always seemed to take turn for the better. In time, I decided to turn my book of notes into a book about using this approach to counseling in working with couples. I wanted to be sure that anyone who was interested in doing solution-focused work with couples could do so without having to overcome the same barriers that I faced along the way. This book, *Solution Building in Couples Therapy,* was released in 2012, and it has been sold all over the world and afforded me the ability to travel and conduct trainings and seminars throughout the U.S. and many other countries. This is the first book that has been written for clinicians to learn to use the solution-focused approach with couples.

When I began this journey, I did not consider myself any kind of relationship expert; I was simply passionate about helping couples and using the solution-focused approach in doing so. The tens and thousands of couples that have come to my office and allowed me the privilege of working with them have taught me everything I have learned and shared in this book. In my time working with couples, I have seen people do the most incredible things to change the direction of their relationships and these interactions with couples have taught me to believe in the power of people and the power of love. In this time, I have observed several trends that the happiest of couples tend to follow which lead to them having successful, lasting relationships.

Specifically, there are five habits that, when practiced, have a long-term impact on a relationship, regardless of the problems that have occurred up until the point of change. This book will review these five habits and will allow readers to practice these habits in their own relationships. Each subsequent chapter will focus on one habit, including exercises and tips that can be used at home to impact the most important relationship in your life ... immediately!

What's in the Book

The book starts with the most foundational idea for any relationship, and the idea upon which the rest of book is based: having a goal for your relationship. Couples that maintain an idea of what type of marriage they are building, and how they would like this marriage to play a role in their lives, tend to have the ability to build towards their vision. In Chapter 2, I discuss the impact of having frequent conversations about the beginning of your relationship. This includes exploring how you initially developed loving feelings and, subsequently, built a relationship that had a future. The following chapter will focus on communication patterns and will demonstrate a more productive way to communicate with your partner. This is an integral step and something that many couples never master. Once learned, the outcome is extraordinary.

The next idea covered is that couples should continue to date. This is by no means a new idea, but this book will present this idea in greater detail and with more clarity to help breathe new life into the old idea of 'keep dating.' Finally, I will illustrate the importance of functioning as a true partnership and how to construct this type of dynamic within your relationship.

Each chapter contains exercises and suggestions on how you can successfully implement the habits in this book into your relationship so that you may experience a positive benefit right away.

One More Thing...

As the name, *Solution Focused Therapy* implies, the focus of this approach is not on the problems with your relationship; it is on the solutions. I have conducted trainings all over the world and, without a doubt, the number one question I get is something like, "How does this approach help couples with (insert problem)?"

The absolute magic of the solution-focused approach is that it operates under the assumption that the root of the problem does not have to be understood in order for the problem to go away. In fact, focusing on the problem usually only serves to make the problem more severe and more long lasting. By doing the things listed in the previous paragraphs, you will be forcing your perceptions to focus on strengths rather than weaknesses, successes rather than failures, and, of course, solutions rather than problems. Why this works will be covered in great detail throughout this book, but I wanted to introduce this concept now to be very clear about these ideas from the onset. This will be a journey toward a new experience for you in your relationship. Perhaps your relationship has recently encountered a traumatic and painful event, such as an affair. Or maybe your relationship has simply fallen into a bit of a rut. Regardless of why you picked up this book, the information contained in these pages will undoubtedly help propel you toward your desired future. As mentioned, I have learned the habits discussed in this book from years of working with thousands of couples and the power of these actions is undeniable.

So, sit back, find a nice, comfortable place to begin this journey and enjoy the ride!

Chapter 1: Have a Goal for Your Relationship

"A goal properly set is halfway reached."

—ZIG ZIGLAR

Imagine getting in a car without knowing where you are going. From the time you start the car and begin to pull out of the parking space, you are already lost. This analogy, with respect to relationship, seems very straightforward and perhaps even too simple. However, the message is quite relevant to most couples.

Establishing a goal — or destination — is arguably the most critical step when trying to accomplish any major task. Yet, most couples start out without ever formulating a clear plan for their future. The beginning of a relationship is an enjoyable time, but often partners can get caught up in the emotions and inadvertently skip the most important step for the beginning of the relationship. In the beginning, people are enjoying the euphoric feelings (rightfully so) and miss the opportunity to examine the relationship when it is at its best. Developing a clear picture of what they would like their relationship to look like in the future is often overlooked.

Through the years of working with couples, I have noticed that partners who spent time in the early stages identifying their goals — both long term, short term and everything in between — tend to be happier and more often on the same page than couples who don't.

Defining "Goal"

I want to be very clear: I do not mean that new couples, once they realize they are compatible, must sit down and have a "business like" meeting to figure out what their future will look like. That would be ridiculous. Instead, I suggest something totally different.

When I got engaged to my wife years ago, I received a gift from one of my aunts that changed the direction of my life. At the time I proposed, I was a recent college graduate and had not yet decided to pursue a graduate degree in counseling. I had no idea that the gift, a book, would make such a difference in my life and marriage. The book was entitled, *The Hard Questions: 100 Questions to Ask Before You Say 'I Do'* by Susan Piver. In truth, this was something of a strange gift for me. I was not much of a reader at that time in my life, and nothing about my fiancée and I at that time suggested that we would benefit from a book like this. I remember opening the package that contained the book and thinking, "what are we supposed to do with this?" The book was placed on a nightstand in my room (at the time we were not living together) and little thought was given to the book after that. Then, one night when we were preparing to go out, my new fiancée suggested that we bring the book and discuss it over dinner. It ended up being a brilliant idea and became a habit we continued for the duration of our year-and-a-half long engagement.

The premise of the book is that each chapter is a series of marriage-related questions that the couple is supposed to answer. In each chapter, the questions are grouped into topics related to the creation of a relationship — sex, family, health, etc. The book is filled with chapters and questions. My future wife and I would spend hours answering these questions, with each question launching us into a detailed conversation about what we would like our future to look like in relation to that question. By the time our wedding day arrived, we had completed the entire book and, as a result, had developed a detailed picture of what our relationship would look like in the future in many different aspects.

We were on the same page about topics such as future plans for children, how we would handle money, how we would decorate our home … the list is endless. We were now aware of each other's deepest thoughts and deepest desires for this relationship. We were able to prepare for the future challenges that awaited us by each of us now understanding how the other felt about those topics. Most importantly, we were able to deepen our friendship and grow closer during an amazing time in our lives.

In addition to the impact on our relationship, reading this book had two other consequences in my life.

First, I began to suggest this book to people close to me. Time after time, whenever someone let me know that they had become engaged, I would explain just how much my wife and I benefited from the book and give it as a gift.

The second effect is quite significant and touched many more people than just those with whom I was able to share the book. One of the key tenets of the solution-focused approach is the therapist inviting clients into conversations that elicit detailed descriptions of their preferred futures. In doing this, clients experience a similar result from what my wife and I experienced in reading the book as we approached our wedding. It was this idea — the idea that our future is more powerful than our past, the idea that the more we were able to identify what we wanted our future to look like that more likely those envisioned descriptions would manifest themselves — that drew me to become a psychotherapist. When I began to have these types of sessions with couples, I noticed the outcomes were overwhelmingly positive and the impact that was being felt on the couples' relationships was nothing short of amazing. Time and time again, a couple would enter therapy with the divorce process already in progress. Sometimes, the couple would be so far into the process of ending the relationship that a divorce was inevitable. Then, just by engaging in conversations about the details of their preferred future, something incredible would transpire. Partners would grow closer and immediately begin to take steps to resolve the relationship and end divorce proceedings.

The Story of Trisha and Tony

Trisha and Tony came to my office seeking pre-marriage counseling to prepare for their wedding, which was coming in six months or so. I quickly realized that pre-marriage counseling was not the only thing that this couple was seeking. Tony had recently discovered that Trisha had been involved in an affair with one of her coworkers. As you can imagine, Tony was devastated and was no longer certain that he could go through with the wedding. During the first session, I asked this couple to describe what type of relationship they would like to create if they decided to stay together. I asked each partner to complete a list. The list would consist of 50 things that would be happening in their future that would signify to them that they had built this relationship in a way that was right for the two of them. This was a very difficult conversation and it was a hard session to conduct.

However, as the list developed, there was a noticeable shift in the mood of the room. The language shifted from being filled with anger, defensiveness and frustration to a language of hope, forgiveness and love. As more and more details of the future were revealed, the more the room changed. It has been several years since this session took place, but I will never forget one of Tony's answers and the impact it had on Trisha. It was clear that Trisha was devastated by her actions in having the affair and she had a significant amount of fear that Tony would never forgive her. Rightfully so, as Tony had been expressing to her that he was not sure if he could ever forgive her. Then, out of nowhere, when the couple reached the mid-30's of their list, Tony said he would like to build a relationship that was filled with forgiveness without rehashing the past. Trisha was stunned and she immediately began to cry. She stated that she would like to build a relationship that was filled with trust and she would work to regain Tony's trust throughout their relationship. The couple immediately embraced and spent the rest of the session in each other's arms.

In the coming weeks, we continued to meet and the couple continued to identify the details of their future. Subsequently, they began to pay more attention to how each person was working to create that future between sessions and no longer focused on the problems they had been experiencing. It was amazing to watch this couple go through this transformation in just a few short weeks!

I am in no way suggesting that this progress was easy; trust me, this couple worked quite hard. I am simply suggesting that once the couple spent time identifying their "goal" for the relationship, then it became more productive for the couple to focus on creating their identified future instead of focusing on getting over past mistakes.

This may seem unusual or even unrealistic, but when you think about it a bit deeper, it makes a lot of sense. You might consider it this way: the human brain is a very complicated organ, but, despite that, it can only hold one thought at a time. Consequently, if you are spending your time focusing on the future, then you physically cannot spend time thinking about the past or the flaws and mistakes of your partner. This new focus leads to a very different experience within the relationship and, thus, changes the potential for the outcome of the relationship.

Conclusion

By spending time developing a goal or future vision for your relationship, I am not proposing that you will be ensuring that your relationship will be free of all problems. I am simply expressing that, by doing this, you will be ensuring that there is an understanding within the relationship that will serve to keep partners on the same page and provide a reference point in a time when things may stray off course a bit. If this step is not taken — and as I mentioned previously, most couples fail to do this — then you are leaving a lot to chance when it comes to how the relationship moves forward. This is simply too big a risk to take when we are trying to do something as monumental as building a happy relationship. Also, by doing this, you force yourselves to notice the best of one another and have conversations about those things, as opposed to only noticing problems.

Exercise

Just as with the aforementioned couple, it is important to develop a defined picture of your preferred future so that both parties understand:

- Exactly what they are building
- The required skills to build it
- How to know when your partner is effectively helping to build it
- When you have successfully accomplished your goal

The first exercise in this book is to develop this type of picture with your partner. So, what I invite you to do is to complete a list of 50 details of what you would like your relationship to look like one year from now. There are a few rules to this exercise.

- The list must be created together.

- Each item added to the list must be presented in a positive and present focused way, e.g. "We won't be fighting" should be changed to "We will be communicating effectively."

- You must get to 50!

Chapter 2: Take Credit for the "Honeymoon" Phase of Your Relationship

"Love is like a friendship caught on fire. In the beginning a flame, very pretty, often hot and fierce, but still only light and flickering. As love grows older, our hearts mature and our love becomes as coals, deep-burning and unquenchable."

—BRUCE LEE

It happened on a normal afternoon during the fall semester. I was walking across the campus on my way from basketball practice. As I was walking, I noticed a beautiful girl standing by her car looking a bit worried. I immediately recognized her as someone that had been in several of my psychology classes. She was very pretty. I will never forget when I saw her that day. She was standing next to her car and there was not another car in the parking lot, as it was late in the afternoon and all of the students and professors had left the campus. There she was, a beautiful girl, and I decided to approach her to find out if she needed help. I asked her if she was okay and she replied by saying that she had left the lights on in her car, killing her battery. She continued to explain that she was waiting for her father, who was an hour away. Since it was getting late, I asked if she would like some company and, luckily, she said yes. During that hour we just talked. Nothing special and certainly not romantic; we just stood by her car and talked.

By the end of the conversation, she offered me her phone number and, of course, I accepted. The funny thing is, she did not mean this as a romantic gesture. It was simply because the conversation was so pleasant she had hoped to continue it. Strangely enough, I also did not accept her phone number with thoughts of dating or anything like that. I, too, was just happy to have met a friend and wanted to continue our chat. Eventually her father showed up, jumped her car and away she went. Little did I know that I had just met my future wife.

I walked away from that conversation feeling so good. In truth, I cannot recall at all what we talked about. It was the start of something special and neither of us knew it. As I was heading back to my dorm, I felt good about myself for the first time in a long time. I had this wonderful girl's phone number in my pocket, but I was not at all thinking about anything other than how nice she was and hoping she made it home. Later that night, I called her to check and see if she made it home safely. When she did not answer the phone, I left her a message expressing my concern. I honestly did not think we would ever talk again, but I was okay with it because I was truly just interested in helping this person. To my surprise, later that night she called me back and the rest is history!

That story is the true and honest love story about how I met my wife. It was the day my life took an amazing turn and things have never been the same. She and I spent the next two years building a great friendship that eventually turned into a wonderful romance. Sharing this story, even now, always brings a huge smile to my face. Each and every time my wife and I talk about the beginning of our relationship we smile, we laugh and we remember just how good for one another we really are.

From the time we first met, we both began to use our talents and skills to build a relationship, even before we realized it was occurring. This relationship did not happen by accident. The two of us contributed to its growth and we did so with great attention and effective use of our respective skills.

The beauty is, every relationship has its own story and each couple has two people, complete with their own set of talents and skills that they use to create their relationship. The truth about relationships is that what you notice manifests itself in the relationship. This simple idea is at the very heart of the *Solution Building in Couples Therapy* approach. The only issue is that most couples do not take credit for the formulation of their relationship. In the beginning of the relationship, things are going so well that that we tend to turn off our brains and simply try to enjoy the ride. However, that is the exact opposite of what we should be doing.

Time and time again, couples come into my office seeking to improve their relationships. When I ask them about recent events that have transpired, couples are prepared to give me detailed descriptions of their problems, but they are not equally prepared to discuss the positives that exist with the same level of detail. This discrepancy is much more than just a minor issue; it is the very oxygen that gives the problem in the relationship life. Couples that are able to spend time focusing on what is good between them, in great detail, tend to have the ability to get through the tough times and enjoy their relationship to a much higher degree.

The Story of Steve and Joanne

Several years ago, I was working with an exceptionally challenging couple. I was a new therapist at the time and this was one of the very first couples with which I had ever worked. Steve, a rough kind of guy, could easily be described as a "man's man." Joanne was quite a fiery woman and it was clear that, though Steve was a rough guy, she was not the type to back down. It was clear when they came into my office that they had both been hurt and subsequently spent time arguing about certain events. When the session got started, the couple resumed their conversation in the argumentative way that had plagued this couple since this problem had begun to interrupt their relationship. It was difficult for me to interrupt the conversation and conduct a therapeutic conversation. It was almost like I was not there. I would pose a question and they would just keep on arguing with one another. As I sat in the session with this couple, I was struggling to find useful questions I could ask, digging for useful words I could say that would shift the focus away from the current problems and towards helpfulness. Then, out of pure desperation, I asked the couple how they met. The response was amazing!

The couple's mood shifted instantaneously, and they told me what, to this day, is the most amazing love story I have ever heard. They described that when they first met they could not keep their eyes, or hands, off of one another. They never fought, always spent time together. They described how they met at a bar and how their eyes met from across the room. They both knew instantly there was something between them and once they started to talk they realized just how special this feeling was. As the details of this story unfolded, Steve and Joanne began to move closer to one another on my couch, as the language they used continued to shift both in tone and in content. I began to ask questions to elicit details about how they played a role in this amazing story (meaning it did not happen by accident). For example, in the beginning of the relationship Steve would make sure that he called Joanne each night just before he went to sleep to ensure she was the last thing on his mind. He commented that this helped him have pleasant thoughts every night and falling asleep while smiling became a common occurrence. Joanne also contributed to the relationship starting off so well. As the relationship was getting started Joanne wanted Steve to know just how much she liked him, so she made it a point every time they saw each other to show him a smile as a sign to him that she was pleased to be with him. These two things may seem small, but if they had not been done, the relationship may not have grown in the great way that it did. Each partner played a role, even though they did not notice it. So, you see how the relationship prospering was neither an accident nor a coincidence. It was the result of two people working well together to create a mutually beneficial environment. The longer we reviewed the "honeymoon phase" of their relationship, the more the couple shifted and actually transformed themselves into the couple that did the work to fall in love rather than the couple that was experiencing problems.

In time, I have come to believe that this kind of transformation makes sense. Imagine that a young child has asked you a question about a particular song that you loved during your youth. In order to answer that question, you have to close your eyes and allow your brain to take you back to a time when the song was meaningful in your life. I'm guessing you may even be feeling the way this particular song used to make you feel all those years ago. This is exactly what happens when we review the details of the successful past of our relationships. It forces our brains to shift back to being the person that constructed the relationship instead of the person that may be unhappy or behaving in destructive ways. It really is that simple.

Conclusion

The message of this chapter is that your relationship's successful past is more important than any current problems. To take that further, the talents that each partner possesses are more important than their flaws. Once understood and applied, these ideas can have a profound impact on your relationship, regardless how severe your current problems may be. The bad news about being a human is that we are all flawed and have personality deficits. However, the absolutely great news is that we also have talents, amazing and wonderful talents. When we learn to live our lives while recognizing and utilizing our talents, those talents have a way of overpowering our flaws, thus resolving even the most difficult of problems. We simply have to shift our perceptions to notice the things that move us in that direction.

Exercise

Get together with your partner and recount to each other the story of how you met. Then answer the following questions:

- What did your partner do that led to the relationship moving forward from the time you first met? List at least 10 per partner.

- What did you notice about your partner that let you know that they were interested in creating a relationship with you? List at least 10 per partner.

- What did you do to let your partner know that you were interested in building a relationship with them? List at least 10 per partner.

- How long were the two of you able to keep the "honeymoon phase" going? How did you keep it going so long? List at least 25 ways you were able to keep this going.

Chapter 3: Communicate About Progress

"It sounds so trite but in relationships, you have to

communicate."

—PETER KRAUSE

Marriage counselors everywhere will agree that communication is one of the most frequently discussed components of a relationship.

Communication ... so simple, yet so important. I am sure that you, the reader, do not need to read another book or hear another lecture about how important communication actually is or how hard we need to work on maintaining it in our relationships.

Instead, I am going to offer a different take on

communicating. Doing so, in this new way requires a simple shift in perception and requires certain changes in what is expressed verbally, the end result allowing us to experience drastic, positive impacts. I must remind you that simple does not always mean easy.

The Solution-Focused Approach in Effective Communication

There is something so special about the beginning of a relationship. At this stage, the two people are communicating at their absolute best, each working equally hard at understanding and being understood and each making a concerted effort to communicate in a way that uplifts the relationship. A couple's natural communication genius is on full display, with the outcome being the successful development of a loving relationship. The issue, then, is not a lack of communication skills, but rather the fact that most couples do not notice or recognize the use of their brilliance in the beginning. Like any skill that we don't even know is there, it may eventually dwindle away.

This being said, relationships should never really require that we learn how to communicate. Rather, there may come a time that we need to reignite our already demonstrated, natural ability to communicate.

Notice and Practice

A couple of questions become obvious: Once lost, can you get these dwindling skills back? If so, how?

The answer comes in two parts: notice and practice.

Notice relates to being sure you notice what is best in your partner, in yourself and in your relationship, then having the ability to make those qualities part of your routine conversation. That is, developing the ability to discuss progress more frequently and with the same acuity that problems are discussed. Practice relates to the fact that this type of conversation, after the initial stage of the relationship, may not continue as naturally and, thus, requires continued effort.

It is so important for couples to have habits that bring the positive into their relationship. This is because problems have a way of forcing us to talk. Whenever something troubling happens we tend to seek out our partner and use the infamous words, "we need to talk." However, whenever something positive happens, we do not always have the same drive to sit down with our partners and have same type of intentional, focused conversation. When one partner is seen looking as if something is bothering them, the other will usually ask the common question, "what's wrong?" However, the opposite end of that spectrum is not equally true. When one partner is seen looking positive or content, the question, "what's right?" is not often posed.

Why not? More positive interactions are what we seek, right? If so, then shouldn't more time be spent on learning about our already-present positives? To me, the answer is a simple "yes." However, for most of us, it is more natural to spend more time trying to understand the problem patterns. This is futile because, if we focus on the problem, that is exactly what we will learn about — the problem. The idea I am putting forth here allows people to shift their focus from being 'problem curious' to 'progress curious.' The outcome is overarching progress that touches all aspects of life.

Progression is more important than regression

In the first couple chapters of this book, one of the ideas expressed was the importance of having a detailed picture of your desired future. Now, the important notion is being able to notice and discuss the clues that demonstrate that you and your partner are making strides towards creating your envisioned relationship. Even when there are signs of regression present, the progress is more important. I want to be very clear: the biggest sign of regression is not nearly as important as the smallest sign of progress and thus, the progress needs our attention. This is yet another area that most couples get backwards. However, once this idea is processed and put in its proper perspective, the outcome is nothing short of amazing.

The Story of Elliott and Carmesia

I am not proud of the fact that I have not always been the best husband. In fact, there have been times when I have been close to the worst.

In the beginning of our marriage my wife and I functioned like a well-oiled machine. She was able to pick up where I left off and I was able to pick up her slack; it was truly a beautiful thing and led to a level of happiness that neither of us had ever dared to imagine. Eventually, we faced a challenge that shook our marriage to its core and it was my wife's ability to notice progress that brought us back together.

It all started when I received a troubling phone call from someone threatening me and everything I had been working for. The details of this phone call are not relevant to this book but what is important is the impact it had on me.

I will never forget that night. Even now, several years later, it feels like it was yesterday. The call was so traumatic that I instantly knew I was going to have a hard time dealing with this situation. The next day I reported the threat to the police and was disappointed to find out that there was nothing they could do. I felt helpless and lost. Eventually, this triggered my mood and psyche to slip into a deep depression that would last for months until the situation came to an end with the arrest and eventual conviction of my tormentor.

During this time, I failed to be the husband I had previously been. I kept the true nature of the situation away from my wife as I did not want to scare her. So through her eyes, she just saw her husband pulling away and behaving strangely. Her enthusiastic husband was now lethargic; her restless husband now spent countless hours in bed and the husband who she knew to be attentive to all of her needs was now totally disconnected. I know now that I should I have shared with her the nature of the situation. She would have been able to support me and she would have understood my behavior better. Unfortunately, I did not tell her until long after the scenario was resolved. Since she did not know what was going on, Carmesia started to grow upset with me. I was unreliable so she stopped depending on me. I was distancing myself from her so she pulled away from me. It was truly the hardest time in our marriage. When the situation that had triggered this whole mess was finally resolved I began to feel better and expected that my wife would go back the way things were. This was not the case. Too much damage had been done by my many months in 'depression land.' It was so hard. I was feeling better and getting back to being myself but she was not responding. We began to question if our marriage could survive. Then one day, Carmesia said something brilliant. She asked me how the couples I see in my office get past difficult times. Before I share with you what my answer was and what happened, I want to point something out here. The moment she posed this question to me I immediately felt hope. It was the first time since this whole thing had begun that I felt this level of hope. I could not wait to answer her question. I explained to her that the way people get beyond difficult times is to notice themselves doing things that demonstrate that things are working out. She was so confused. She is not a counselor so I had to explain to her a bit about what I meant. I expounded that this idea meant that if we noticed ourselves moving forward and taking steps to rebuild our relationship then we were more likely to take these steps and experience the subsequent positive outcome.

She was skeptical, but agreed. We began to notice each other resuming our old ways of working together, spending time together and being connected. We would be sure to talk to one another about the fact that we were progressing and learning to depend on one another again.

Sharing stories about my marriage — especially this story — is hard for me, but I want people learn. I passionately want people to know that relationships are a work in progress and how we go about doing that work will decide whether your relationship thrives or perishes. Trust me when I tell you, there is always hope, there is always love. The choice is yours to notice the presence of hope and love so that those parts can reestablish themselves in your relationship.

Conclusion

Of all of the chapters, this may be the most important. In my years in this profession, I cannot count how many couples have expressed to me the power of addressing their communication in this way. Sometimes people are shocked that the problems begin to lose potency and eventually remove themselves from the relationship, just by simply spending time focusing on the positives of the relationship. Like everything else in this book, this is a simple, yet powerful idea.

Exercise

For this exercise, you will not need to write

anything down. The idea here is for this to be interactional. Each day, preferably in the evening or at the end of your day, get with your partner and have a conversation about what each of you is noticing about the other that is pleasing to you. There are a few rules for this talk.

- The conversation must last at least 10 minutes.

- The examples of positives/progress must be recent (within the last few days, or even hours).

- If there is something negative to discuss, it must be held off until after this exercise is completed.

Chapter 4: Continue to Date

"Keep love in your heart. A life without it is like a sunless garden when the flowers are dead."

—OSCAR WILDE

I still remember the night my best friend and his future wife began to date ... and it was over 20 years ago. Before I get to the events of that night, I will need to give a bit of a back-story to our friendship.

When I was young, my family moved from one side of town to another when my parents separated. On the day that we moved, while unloading boxes into the new place, I noticed a kid who looked about my age playing basketball in his backyard. I recognized this kid as someone that I had played baseball against in the town's youth league but I did not know him very well. The next day in school I made sure to find him at the end of the school day to see if he would like to walk home with me. Neither of us knew it at the time, but this was the beginning of a life long friendship that could better be described as a brotherhood.

By the time I made it to my senior year in high school, Kyle and I had been best friends for several years, spending literally every day together. We had gone on vacations together, been through each other's difficult times together and our friendship continued to grow and grow. No two people have ever been closer. That is until one winter night.

Like typical teenagers, Kyle and I spent most weekends hanging out with friends and going to parties. On this particular night, there was a group of very pretty girls from a neighboring town that was attending a party at a friend of ours and Kyle instantly noticed one of the girls. Over the next few weeks he would talk to me about her until he openly confided in me that he was quite interested in this girl, Jenny. Soon after, I ran into Jenny at a mutual friend's house and told her that Kyle was very interested in her. She looked excited and divulged to me that she, too, had noticed Kyle. I gave her his phone number and urged her to call him.

Very quickly, Kyle and Jenny began a serious relationship. I noticed something in him change immediately. There was happiness in his life that I had not seen before. I was having a hard time because I was not hanging out with him as much as previously, but the happiness I would see on his face made the adjustment easier for me. We are still best friends to this day and I have watched him, over the course of the last nearly-20 years, focus on making Jenny happy. I can honestly tell you he looks at her today the same way he looked at her then. Her smile means as much to him today as it did to him then. They now have a wonderful family and the strength of their relationship has produced three of the happiest and most amazing kids.

In the years since they have gotten together, I have moved across the country so I obviously don't get to see them very often. Each time I do see them, I can't help but think of the teenagers who once met and how they have managed to maintain that mentality.

What does this have to do with dating?

Perhaps the most common advice given by marriage counselors is to keep dating. However, in this chapter we will dig a bit deeper into this issue. Most people understand this advice as an act, meaning go on actual "dates." However, I suggest that dating should be viewed as more of a mindset. Kyle and Jenny have found a way to maintain this mindset where they both look at one another with a look of love, they talk about each other with the softness of love and they act with the other's happiness in mind. This is the very essence of the dating mentality.

In the beginning of a relationship, we are carefully selecting words and actions that will result in the happiness of the partner, as well as the overall growth of the relationship. I have watched Kyle and Jenny go from their first date to now, over a decade of marriage. I have seen that they still think and act today the way they did in the beginning. I have not said a word about how often they actually go out on "dates" because that is not the point. They may date weekly or monthly or in some other interval, but I am sure that, daily, he looks at her and behaves in a way that increases the likelihood that they will experience happiness and joy, and she does the same. I once read a quote by Aristotle that says, "Being in love is one soul that exists in two people." This is never truer than in the lives of two people who remember to maintain the "dating" relationship.

A word of caution

The caution, it should be noted, is that your romantic relationship is the easiest relationship in your life to neglect, mostly because your romantic relationship is the one in your life with the least amount of immediacy. What I mean by this is that every other relationship in your life that gets neglected has immediate and severe consequences. For example, if you go to work and do nothing, chances are you will hear from your boss very quickly. If you neglect your job as a parent, your children will immediately respond in a way that shows you that they have suffered. But, if you falter in your relationship, your partner will usually just bury that feeling until they cannot stand it any longer. This can take years and years and is the very reason why, when a partner says he or she is unhappy, another partner is often shocked. They did not know there was a problem because nothing was said and the consequences were not immediate. This allows problem patterns to persist in a romantic relationship in a way that they would not persist in other types of relationships.

As I mentioned earlier in this book, problems make us talk and happiness does not. So, this is another area of your relationship that requires that you create a habit that involves successes and the dating mentality.

The story of David and Sue

There is no power in relationships than the power of dating — not just the act of dating, but the mentality of dating. The one couple I met that most exemplified this over the years was David and Sue. This was a couple that had been divorced for four years when they decided to seek marriage counseling. I later learned that the only reason they came to the session was because a friend on theirs had seen me previously and said that I could

"work miracles." This was quite a compliment but I was

unsure why two people who had been divorced would be

seeking counseling. David and Sue were in their late 40's

and had three children, none of them living at home. The

couple had struggled to co-parent as they did not get

along the majority of the time and the marriage had

ended under very difficult circumstances that involved

infidelity by both partners and lots of hurtful words. It is

quite rare that a couple comes to my office already

divorced but from my perspective, my job was still the

same: ask questions that would elicit the couple's best

hopes for the session(s) and get a detailed description of

what their lives would look like after the problems in the

lives and relationship were solved.

In short order the couple began to get along better

and lots of positive feelings towards each other began to

resurface. In one session David stated that he was

beginning to have feelings for Sue that he had not experienced in years and was not sure what to do with them. It was clear that he was nervous and scared that he would be rejected by Sue or worse — what if they got back together and ended up hurting each other again?

I was stunned at the turn the conversation had just taken. This was the fourth session and from my understanding the couple was seeking to get along as ex-spouses. How did we get here? Well, I will try to explain.

In the previous sessions I had been asking questions related to how they fell in love and what would happen if those forces took over again in their lives. The thinking is if you once had the skills to get along in a romantic relationship then those same skills can play a role in them getting along as ex-spouses. It just did not happen that way. Describing the positive past can be a powerful thing that literally transports our minds into that past. For example, has anyone ever asked you a question such as, "when did that song come out?" In order to answer such a question, we must transport ourselves to the time when the song in question played a role in our lives and we experience a jolt of positivity as a result. Let me use a specific example to make this point. Not too long ago I was driving with my 13-year old nephew in the car with me. A song came on the radio that I had not heard in years, he asked me when the song came out and I began to think. It happened to be the theme song to a movie that my childhood best friend and I used to watch frequently as kids. As I recalled the date, it was as if I was becoming young again and a flood of positive feelings came over me. This is because when our brains focus on something positive the result is a positive feeling. Relationships are the same.

As David and Sue recalled the way they built their relationship, the mentality of the beginning of their relationship returned. The dating mentality they had in the beginning reappeared. Several times they made statements such as, "we haven't thought about this in years" or "I have never described this before."

Soon after David admitted to having feelings for Sue once again, she expressed that she was interested as well. They eventually began to date and were able to maintain that dating mentality until they eventually remarried. I still meet with this couple from time to time to ensure that they always focus on making one another happy and continue to take care of their relationship.

One day, one of the couple's children came to my office to thank me for repairing the family. The family is now back together and the all of the three children feel like they are witnessing a miracle!

Conclusion

The message here is that, in the beginning of the relationship, each partner took the necessary steps to create a relationship that could grow. Unless a habit is developed and actions maintained to keep those feelings, they will likely dissipate over time, sometimes causing irreparable problems. But, like most problems, the solution is not entirely complicated and has an extremely positive and long-lasting outcome.

Exercise

Since the goal here is to reconnect with the dating mentality, this exercise is geared towards reestablishing these habits.

Each partner should do something, in secret, for the other partner daily. The goal here is simple: make your partner smile. Then, simply observe for the presence of their smiles.

Chapter 5: Function as a Partnership

"Friendship is essentially a partnership."

—ARISTOTLE

From the time I was a graduate student learning about counseling, professors would tell me that couples need to learn how to manage money, family issues and sex in order to have effective relationships. Conversations about such sensitive topics, such as money, sex and family can be difficult and can quickly dissolve into arguments, which can only feed feelings of resentment and hostility. I spent many hours thinking about this and how I would, one day, be able to help couples as a marriage therapist.

In time, I learned that my graduate professors

were absolutely right. As I started to work with couples, I noticed that most of them came to my office with the aforementioned issues—money, sex, family. However, I was not yet confident in my ability to be helpful. I began to really focus on finding the best ways to be helpful. I read book after book and attended every lecture I could find. This was somewhat helpful, but I had not yet learned to seek advice from the greatest teachers of all: the couples themselves.

The more and more couples I worked with, the more and more I noticed a simple yet magnificent trend. Couples who recognized and honed their respective skills as partners tended to have fewer problems. To some degree, all couples use these skills. I noticed that, through the process of therapy, as things improved for the couple, the strength of their partnership became enhanced, even if certain issues were not discussed in session.

I want to take a minute to fully explain what I mean by "partnership."

All people have strengths and weaknesses. The trick to having a strong partnership is to use your strengths to overcome your partner's weaknesses and allow you partner's strengths to overcome your own weaknesses. Whether the partnership is in business or in your personal life, this is the essence of an effective relationship. For most people, this concept can be hard to grasp and at the same time be very humbling ... for several reasons. First, even though most people would not argue that we all have strengths and weaknesses, most of us are more aware of our weaknesses than we are our strengths. Thus, we have a limited ability to maximize our strengths for the simple fact that we are not as aware of what our strengths are and what their the true power they possess. I have said many times that if people were as aware of their abilities as they were of their weaknesses, the field of counseling would be obsolete. The point of my therapy, and this entire book, is to help people to become more aware of their strengths—the very best of themselves so that they may use this awareness to live their lives to the fullest and enhance the way they would relate to their partner.

Aside from being largely unaware of strengths, creating a strong partnership is also a challenge because many people have a tendency to do what they are comfortable with rather than doing what actually works. Take my wife and I, for example. When we first got married, we began to have conversations about how we would handle our money and who would be the one in our relationship that would be responsible for paying the bills. This was a challenge because my wife is a very independent woman, and she had always been in control of her own money. Even sharing control was not something she was too excited to do. We were planning to make our first home purchase in the next few years and needed to prepare for that process immediately. Between the two of us, at the time, I was clearly the one that was the most meticulous and, thus, would not allow any of our bills to be paid late, hurting our credit in the process. Reluctantly, she agreed to allow me to be the one to manage our money. In the subsequent years, we accomplished all of the financial goals we set, including the purchase of our first home. We did not have a single argument about money in this time, literally not one. However, that did not last. In time, I decided to open my first counseling office, and it took significant time and a significant amount of my attention away from home. I began to make mistakes in my management of our home finances. I missed bills that should have been paid and we were not able to save the same amount of money as we had previously. One night, my wife and I were having a rather heated conversation about money when we realized our strengths had shifted and, thus, we needed to shift our responsibilities. In the beginning, when I had I a typical '9-to-5' job, I could spend a large amount of time making sure our home finances were in order. Once I opened my counseling office, I began to work 12- to 14-hour days and no longer had the time nor the energy to do as good a job managing our finances. Also, in the beginning of our relationship, my wife had just started graduate school, and now, as my life got busier, her life relaxed a bit due to her graduation. We decided that she would be the one to now manage our home finances and it has been one of the best decisions we have made. In the time since we have made this change, we have once again returned to our typical way of functioning, with no more arguing about money!

We could have both been stubborn, as, in truth, we both enjoy being in control. She had the time that I did not, and she now had the ability to focus on the home in a way that I did not. It was time for me to put my ego aside, move away from what was comfortable, and move towards what would work. It was that simple.

When couples are able to prioritize what is best for them rather than what is comfortable, the outcome is an efficient system and an effective relationship dynamic that brings out the best of both partners. One of the best things about my job as a psychotherapist is watching couples who once thought that they were not good for one another realize that they, in fact, have always possessed the ability to work together. They had merely forgotten to develop roles in the household, based on each partner's strengths, which would lead towards a successful partnership.

Exercise

For this exercise, the goal is to develop roles that each of you will perform in the home based on each partner's strengths. Have a meeting between you and your partner. This meeting will have three parts:

- Develop a list of strengths for each partner that is at least 10 items long.
- Develop a list of household goals.
- Develop a plan for achieving these goals that utilizes the strengths of each partner.

This meeting should be conducted on a monthly basis to review progress and to see if any new goals need to be established. Also, determine whether any circumstances have changed that may require the roles be adjusted. There is one rule, and this rule *must* be followed. No problem talk during this meeting. If a problem is to be discussed, it must wait until after the meeting — not before and not during.

Conclusion

"Love is life's end, but never ending. Love is life's wealth, never spent, but ever spending. Love's is life's reward, rewarded in rewarding."

—HERBERT SPENCER

Thank you!

I have to thank you for allowing me to share the lessons I have learned and the magic that I have witnessed in my years of working with couples.

This book has been a very personal journey for me and I hope that the ideas put forth have been helpful to you and in your relationship. If there is one thing I have grown to believe in, it is the power of two people in love.

I do not believe love ever dies. Just like a never-ending flame, it burns throughout our lives and withstands the trials and tribulations that come our way. I have had several couples come to my office, where one or both partners claimed to no longer be in love, only to experience a total rebirth of emotions in just a short amount of time. I do not believe that, in these instances, love was reignited, rather, I believe the small flame that still existed was simply refueled so that it could become a raging inferno once again. That is the meaning of *The Solution Focused Marriage*. Put simply, it is building a marriage that is infused with habits that help build up each partner, highlight their strengths and make their weaknesses insignificant. *The Solution Focused Marriage* is a marriage that is built on conversations about progress instead of plagued with conversations about problems. The habits in this book were geared to lead towards this type of relationship.

I have been able to listen to the most amazing love stories in my time as a therapist, and the lessons I have learned have been invaluable. It has helped me grow as a professional, but it has also helped me in my own relationship with my wife.

I hope that now you are more aware of your strengths, along with your partner's strengths, and have gained some tools that help you grow these changes into new habits.

You are stronger than your problems.

You are better than your mistakes.

The successes in your life are far more important than your failures. Please don't ever forget it.

About the Author

 Elliott Connie is a psychotherapist that practices in Keller, Texas. He is also the founder and owner of the Solution Focused Training Institute and The Uptown Counseling and Family Therapy Center in Dallas, Texas. He has worked with thousands of couples and families applying the solution focused approach to help them move their lives from the current problems towards their desired futures. He has is the founder and director of The Connie Institute, an organization that conducts trainings for clinicians interested in using the Solution Focused Approach with couples as well as developing training materials. He has traveled the world speaking at national and international conferences in such places as throughout the United States, the United Kingdom, Canada, and Asia training practitioners to apply solution focused principles and techniques in their work. He was also the co-editor of the book entitled *The Art of Solution Focused Therapy* and his second book entitled *Solution Building in Couples Therapy* was released in the Fall of 2012. He is currently working on a research project, along with other leaders in the solution focused community, to define and explore the meaning and process of solution building. He was mentored by noted authors and practicioners such as Bill O'Hanlon, Chris Iveson and Linda Metcalf.

Made in the USA
Monee, IL
19 November 2020

48548033R00059